# Space
# Exploration

By Steve Parker

Illustrated by Alex Pang

Miles Kelly

First published in 2009 by Miles Kelly Publishing Ltd
Bardfield Centre, Great Bardfield, Essex, CM7 4SL

Copyright © Miles Kelly Publishing Ltd 2009

This edition printed in 2009

10 9 8 7 6 5 4 3 2

**Editorial Director:** *Belinda Gallagher*
**Art Director:** *Jo Brewer*
**Design Concept:** *Simon Lee*
**Volume Design:** *Rocket Design*
**Cover Designer:** *Simon Lee*
**Indexer:** *Gill Lee*
**Production Manager:** *Elizabeth Brunwin*
**Reprographics:** *Stephan Davis, Ian Paulyn*
**Consultants:** *John and Sue Becklake*

ISBN 978-1-84810-119-7

Printed in China

British Library Cataloguing-in-Publication Data
A catalogue record for this book is available from
the British Library

MADE WITH PAPER FROM
A SUSTAINABLE FOREST

## ACKNOWLEDGEMENTS

All panel artworks by Rocket Design
The publishers would like to thank the following
sources for the use of their photographs:
**Corbis:** 9 Bettman; 13 Roger Ressmeyer
**Rex Features:** 15 Everett Collection; 25 Denis Cameron;
33 Sipa Press; 35 Scaled Composites
**Science Photo Library:** 6; 11 Ria Novosti;
21 NASA; 29 European Space Agency; 37 NASA
All other photographs are from NASA and
Miles Kelly Archives

## WWW.FACTSFORPROJECTS.COM

Each top right-hand page directs
you to the Internet to help you
find out more. You can log on
to **www.factsforprojects.com**
to find free pictures, additional
information, videos, fun activities
and further web links. These
are for your own personal use
and should not be copied or
distributed for any commercial
or profit-related purpose.

If you do decide to use the
Internet with your book, here's a
list of what you'll need:
• A PC with Microsoft® Windows®
  XP or later versions, or a
  Macintosh with OS X or later,
  and 512Mb RAM

• A browser such as Microsoft®
  Internet Explorer 7, Firefox 2.X
  or Safari 3.X
• Connection to the Internet via
  a modem (preferably 56Kbps) or
  a faster Broadband connection
• An account with an Internet
  Service Provider (ISP)
• A sound card for listening to
  sound files

**Links won't work?**
**www.factsforprojects.com** is
regularly checked to make sure
the links provide you with lots
of information. Sometimes you
may receive a message saying
that a site is unavailable. If this
happens, just try again later.

**Stay safe!**
When using the Internet, make
sure you follow these guidelines:
• Ask a parent's or a guardian's
  permission before you log on.
• Never give out your personal
  details, such as your name,
  address or email.
• If a site asks you to log in or
  register by typing your name
  or email address, speak to your
  parent or guardian first.
• If you do receive an email from
  someone you don't know, tell
  an adult and do not reply to the
  message.
• Never arrange to meet anyone
  you have talked to on the
  Internet.

Miles Kelly Publishing is not
responsible for the accuracy or
suitability of the information on
any website other than its own.
We recommend that children are
supervised while on the Internet
and that they do not use Internet
chat rooms.

*www.mileskelly.net*

*info@mileskelly.net*

# CONTENTS

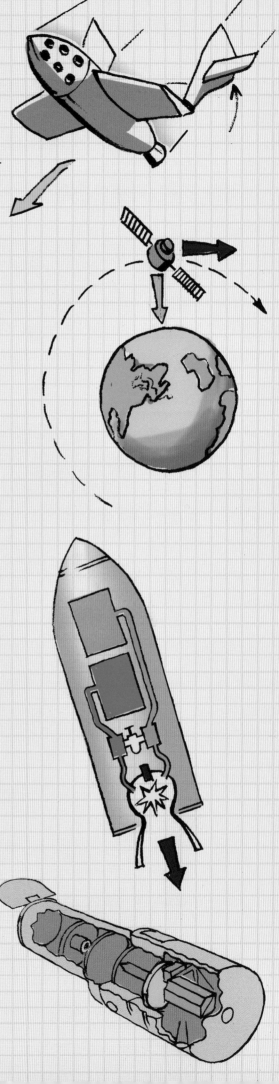

# INTRODUCTION

Long ago there were no street lamps, electric lights or even candles, just glowing wood fires. Ancient humans had time to look up at the Moon, planets, stars and other twinkling specks in the night sky. Legends grew about gods and spirits in a mysterious dark world far above. From 1610, the telescope made these tiny specks bigger. Astronomers realized that they were faraway worlds moving through a vast, empty area called 'space'.

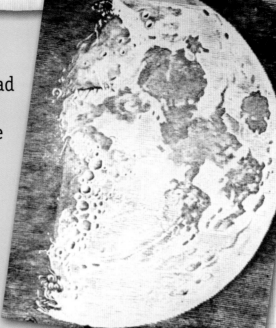

In 1635, Claude Melan drew the first detailed telescopic map of the Moon.

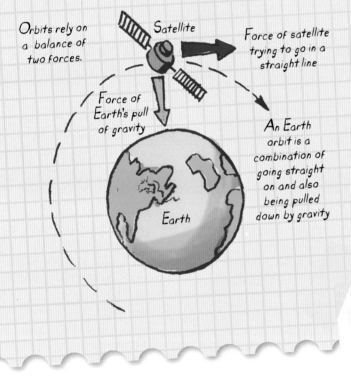

Orbits rely on a balance of two forces.

Satellite

Force of satellite trying to go in a straight line

Force of Earth's pull of gravity

An Earth orbit is a combination of going straight on and also being pulled down by gravity

Earth

## INTO ORBIT

In the early 1900s, Russian schoolteacher Konstantin Tsiolkovsky suggested how a machine called a rocket could escape Earth's pull of gravity and go into orbit – an 'endless fall' round and round our planet. In the 1920s, American engineer Robert Goddard made a practical start with the first controllable rockets. World War II (1939–1945) saw the first big long-distance rocket, the V-2. Designed as a weapon of destruction, it was the first man-made object to reach space (a height above 100 kilometres).

## SPACE RACE

The 1950s 'Cold War' was a trial of strength between the two world superpowers, the USA and USSR. In this 'Space Race' the USSR scored three great firsts – an orbiting satellite, an orbiting human and an orbiting space station. The USA followed a longer-term goal and developed the most powerful rocket ever, Saturn V. It sent the first humans to another world, when Apollo 11 landed on the Moon in 1969.

Saturn V rockets took eight Apollo spacecraft to the Moon between 1968 and 1972, with six landings.

The spacecraft featured in this book are Internet linked.
Visit www.factsforprojects.com to find out more.

*First person on the Moon, Neil Armstrong, is reflected in the visor of the second person and photographer, Buzz Aldrin.*

## SATURN LANDING

In 2004, seven years after launch, the Cassini-Huygens probe reached Saturn. The Huygens lander detached from the Cassini orbiter and parachuted down to Saturn's giant moon Titan – an automatic process that went without a hitch.

*Huygen's descent onto Titan*

*Heat shield prevented burn-up on entry into Titan's atmosphere*

*Large parachute and then a smaller one slowed Huygen's decent*

*Huygens lands on Titan*

*The International Space Station is a temporary workplace for dozens of scientists – and a hotel for the occasional space tourist.*

## SPACE GETS BUSY

Today, trips to the International Space Station (ISS) grab the headlines. However space probes travel much further. They visit all the planets going around our Sun, many of their moons and smaller objects such as asteroids and comets. Their findings help us to understand how and when the Universe began. Much nearer and more practical for our daily lives are hundreds of satellites orbiting Earth. They provide television links, telephone calls and computer communications, help us to forecast the weather, monitor global warming and carry out spying missions.

*Space is not as empty as it was 50 years ago. What will the next 50 years bring?*

# V-2 ROCKET

The V-2 missile was the first big long-distance rocket. Its earliest flight was in 1942 in the middle of World War II (1939–1945). After the war the V-2 was the first rocket to reach space, but it never went into orbit around the Earth. Almost all space rockets that followed the V-2 were based on its design.

## Eureka!

The first rockets used gunpowder as fuel. Called 'fire arrows', they were invented in China around AD 1050. The first rocket with liquid fuel was launched by Robert Goddard in 1926. It reached a height of just 12 metres!

## Whatever next?

The USA plans a 'Star Wars' network of satellites in space to detect enemy missiles so counter-attack missiles can be fired at them.

**Warhead**  The nose cone was filled with three-quarters of a tonne of the explosive Amatol, based on TNT (trinitrotoluene).

Nose cone

Fuel tank

Oxidizer tank

Pump for fuel and oxidizer

Igniter sets fire to fuel

Combustion chamber where fuel burns

Nozzle

In 1951 a V-2 blasted to a record height of 213 km. That's well into space, which officially starts at 100 km.

**Controls**  Early V-2s steered themselves on a preset course. Later versions were controlled by radio signals from the ground.

## ✳ How do ROCKET ENGINES work?

Burning gases provide thrust

Rockets use the basic scientific law of action-reaction. As burning gases from the rocket engine blast out backwards, they push the rocket forwards. Burning needs oxygen, but space has no air and therefore no oxygen. Rockets take liquid oxygen or an oxygen-rich chemical called an oxidizer.

Just after launch the V-2 used 'gas rudders' just below the nozzle for steering. By the time the V-2 was going fast enough, the air vanes on the fins also began to work as rudders.

**Fuel tank**  The upper tank contained nearly 4 tonnes of a mixture of liquids. Three-quarters was ethanol, a type of alcohol that burns well but at extremely high temperatures. The rest was water, to make the burning temperature slightly lower.

*Discover more facts about the V-2 Rocket by visiting www.factsforprojects.com and clicking on the web link.*

The V-2's rocket engine only ran for about 65 seconds but this was enough to reach a height of 80 km. It fell back to Earth and exploded up to 300 km away from the launch site.

## ✳ Launching the V-2

The V-2 blasted off from a special steel launch pad shaped like a low table. This and all the other equipment required were carried by about 30 trucks to the launch site, usually hidden among trees in a forest. The V-2 itself had a special truck and trailer almost 15 metres long, weighing 11 tonnes. The launch crew took 90 minutes to set up the platform, prepare the V-2 and its fuel and guidance systems and then arm (switch on) the explosive warhead.

*A V-2 rocket being prepared for launch*

Streamlined body

Fuel pumps

**Combustion chamber** The fuel sprayed into this chamber through more than 1200 tiny nozzles, where it burnt using the oxygen.

Air vane

**Liquid oxygen tank** The lower tank carried almost 5 tonnes of oxygen. This was so cold and under such immense pressure that it was squeezed into a liquid rather than being a gas.

Fuel for fuel pump

Nozzle

Fin

During World War II more than 3000 V-2s were launched at enemies.

# SPUTNIK 1

On 4 October 1957 the world was stunned by amazing news – the first satellite in space. Sputnik 1 was launched by an R-7 Semyorka rocket into orbit around the Earth. It was the first of many Sputniks to test new machines and technologies in space. It lasted three months, then burned up as it fell back to Earth.

## Eureka!

An orbiting comsat (communications satellite) receives and sends out radio signals as if it was on an incredibly tall mast. The first person to have the idea for comsats was science fiction writer Arthur C Clarke (1917–2008) way back in 1945.

Sputnik 1 sent out radio signals for 22 days before its batteries died. However it continued for a total of 1440 orbits and a total journey of 60 million km.

**O-ring** A ring-shaped joint between the inner casing halves sealed the satellite to keep in its contents of pure nitrogen gas.

## ✳ How do ORBITS work?

An orbit is the curved path of an object, such as a satellite, around a planet, moon or star. It is a balance between moving forwards and falling downwards. In space, an object tends to go straight on unless a force affects it. Earth's gravity causes a force – a pull that makes the object curve around, as if falling. However the Earth's surface also curves around below the object. If the object's speed and height are exactly right, it keeps 'falling' but never reaches the ground.

**Power supply**
The three small but heavy batteries weighed as much as a small adult person. Two were for the radio transmitter and one was for the fan to control the temperature inside.

Inner casing

Object tries to go straight on

Pull of gravity

An orbit is a combination of going straight on and being pulled down

Earth

Ventilation fan

One month after Sputnik 1 was launched, Sputnik 2 carried the first space passenger – Laika the dog.

EXPLODED VIEW

## Whatever next?

There are more than 600 working satellites in space, hundreds more 'dead' ones and thousands of old bits of rockets, space stations and other space junk. Each new satellite is given an orbit to help it avoid all of these existing objects.

To listen to Sputnik's radio beeps in space visit www.factsforprojects.com and click on the web link.

Sputnik 1 was launched by the USSR, which is now Russia and nearby nations. Their big space rival the USA was very surprised and some Americans thought the news was a trick!

**Outer casing** The two halves of the ball-shaped casing were made of an alloy (metal mixture) of aluminium, magnesium and titanium fixed together with 36 bolts.

Sputnik 1 started the Space Age by showing that machines, and maybe even people, could go into orbit and survive.

**Antennae** The four antennae, or aerials, which sent out the radio signals were made of thin 'whips' more than 2 metres long.

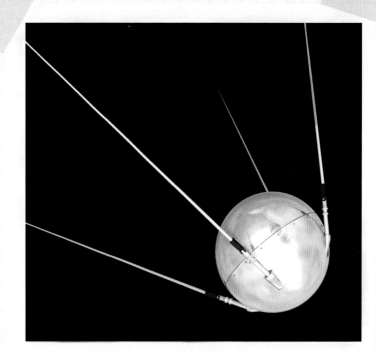

Sputnik 1 weighed 84 kg and was 58 cm across – about the size of a big beachball.

Sputnik 1's single transmitter weighed 3.7 kilograms. It sent out two sets of radio signal beeps, low and high, each 0.3 seconds long.

Inner casing

Heat resistant outer casing

## ✴ What is ESCAPE VELOCITY?

If you could launch a spacecraft into the air, Earth's pull of gravity would soon bring it back down. The harder you launch it, the higher it goes but it would never reach very far. A rocket is the only engine powerful enough to give a spacecraft enough movement energy to break free of Earth's gravity and get into space. At Earth's surface this means a speed of 11 kilometres per second, which is known as the escape velocity.

The R-7 rocket blasts off with Sputnik 1 in its nose cone

# EXPLORER 1

A fter the shock of seeing its rival the USSR launch Sputnik 1 (see page 10), the USA increased its efforts to send its first satellite into space. Four months later on 31 January 1958, Explorer 1 blasted off from Cape Canaveral, inside the nose of a Juno I rocket. During its 111-day mission, Explorer 1 made several exciting discoveries about conditions in space.

## Eureka!

Explorer 1 found a doughnut-shaped region of tiny particles trapped around Earth by the planet's natural magnetic field. The region was named the Van Allen Belt after James Van Allen, one of the Explorer mission leaders.

## Whatever next?

The Explorer series of satellites carried on until 1981 when Explorer 59 studied how sunlight and polluting gases form smog.

Explorer 1's orbit was elliptical, or oval, in shape. 2550 km above Earth at its farthest but only 360 km at its nearest.

## ✳ How do MULTI-STAGE ROCKETS work?

A multi-stage rocket, or launch vehicle, is several rockets on top of one another. The first stage is biggest and most powerful because it has the greatest weight to lift. Also, it sets off from the ground where Earth's gravity is strongest. After it uses up its fuel it falls away, or separates. The whole launch vehicle is now lighter and higher, so gravity is weaker. This means the second stage can be smaller, and so on.

Second stage: This needs less power and fuel to keep going

Separation

First stage: This uses its fuel and then falls away, otherwise it would be 'dead weight'

Fuel tank

Oxidizer tank

Rocket engine

### Cosmic ray detector
A tube-shaped detector measured the strength of cosmic rays. These are like radio waves but each one is much shorter in length.

### High-power transmitter
The two transmitters sent information from the onboard sensors and detectors down to Earth as radio signals.

Metal casing

### Temperature sensors
There were five temperature sensors – one in the nose, one in the main body and three on the outside.

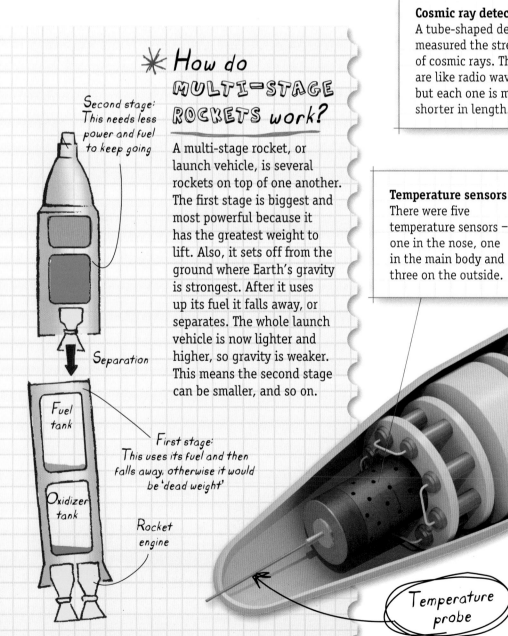

Based on the metal mercury, the batteries made up two-fifths of Explorer 1's payload weight.

Temperature probe

Discover more about Explorer 1 and the start of the Space Race by visiting www.factsforprojects.com and clicking on the web link.

Nozzle

**Antennae** Four short whip-like antennae (aerials) on the outside, plus two straight antennae built into the satellite casing, sent out radio signals.

Explorer 1 was 15 cm wide and at 14 kg, it was only one-sixth of the weight of Sputnik 1.

Fibre-glass ring

At 203 cm long, Explorer 1 was not much taller than an adult

Explorer 1 was the first satellite to use newly invented transistors, which helped to control the satellite's electronics, and also made it much lighter than using older devices called valves.

To the surprise of mission experts, when Explorer 1 got into orbit it changed the direction in which it spun – 12 times each second. No one knew why.

## ✳ TRACKING STATIONS

As rockets, satellites, probes and other craft travel through space they send back to Earth all kinds of information about where they are and what they have found. The information is sent in the form of radio signals. Huge dishes on Earth detect the weak signals and swivel to point at, or track, the spacecraft as they move across the sky. As the Earth spins around once every 24 hours, different tracking stations take turns around the world.

Parkes Observatory tracking station, Australia

# VOSTOK 1

The first person in space was Yuri Gagarin, a Russian pilot-turned-astronaut, on the mission known as Vostok 1. On 12 April 1961 he made one orbit of Earth in his Vostok 3KA spacecraft. The trip lasted just one hour 48 minutes. It made Gagarin a hero and started the era of human space travel.

## Eureka!

As far back as 1903, Russian scientist Konstantin Tsiolkovskii wrote about using rockets to reach space and that one day people might travel there. Others at the time thought he was mad!

**Hatch** The door into the craft was sealed after the astronaut went in. It was released after re-entry to allow Gagarin to bail out with his parachute.

*The Vostok team's radio call sign for Gagarin's craft was 'Swallow', and for Yuri himself 'Cedar'.*

**Descent module** Only the ball-shaped part of the craft containing the astronaut came back to Earth.

**Visor** The Visor (Vzor) was like a window-mounted periscope (angled telescope). It helped to position the craft in the correct position and angle for re-entry.

## ✳ How does RE-ENTRY work?

One of the riskiest parts of a return mission is re-entry, when the craft comes back from empty space down into Earth's atmosphere – the layer of air around the planet. At a speed of 10 kilometres each second, rubbing, or friction, with the thickening air rapidly makes the craft glow red-hot. The key is to enter at the right angle. Otherwise the craft skips off the atmosphere like a stone bouncing off a pond's surface, or plunges too steeply to a fiery end.

Overshoot zone

Re-entry corridor

Undershoot zone

*Entry too steep, craft overheats into a fireball*

*Entry too shallow, craft bounces off atmosphere into deep space*

**Ejector seat** Explosives blew Gagarin and his seat out of the craft, ready to open his parachute.

To watch a video of Yuri Gagarin blasting into space visit
www.factsforprojects.com and click on the web link.

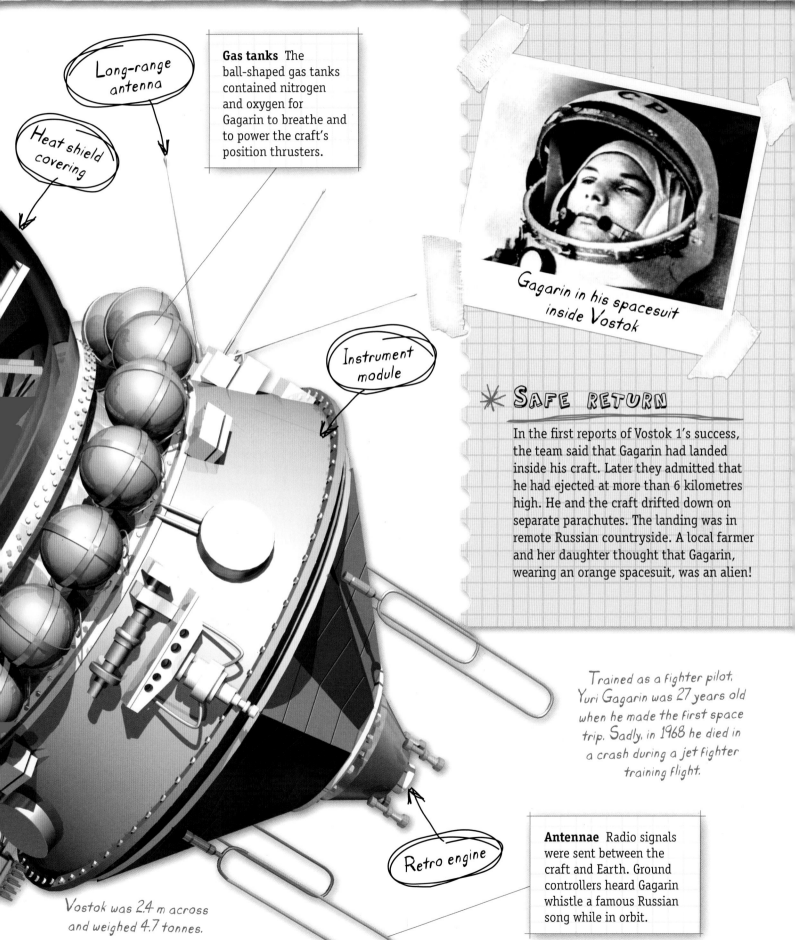

Long-range antenna

Heat shield covering

**Gas tanks** The ball-shaped gas tanks contained nitrogen and oxygen for Gagarin to breathe and to power the craft's position thrusters.

Instrument module

Retro engine

Vostok was 2.4 m across and weighed 4.7 tonnes.

Gagarin in his spacesuit inside Vostok

## ✳ SAFE RETURN

In the first reports of Vostok 1's success, the team said that Gagarin had landed inside his craft. Later they admitted that he had ejected at more than 6 kilometres high. He and the craft drifted down on separate parachutes. The landing was in remote Russian countryside. A local farmer and her daughter thought that Gagarin, wearing an orange spacesuit, was an alien!

Trained as a fighter pilot, Yuri Gagarin was 27 years old when he made the first space trip. Sadly, in 1968 he died in a crash during a jet fighter training flight.

**Antennae** Radio signals were sent between the craft and Earth. Ground controllers heard Gagarin whistle a famous Russian song while in orbit.

# SATURN V

The biggest and most powerful rocket to take craft into space was the USA's Saturn V. It launched Apollo astronauts on their journeys to the Moon. From the first Apollo test flight in November 1969 to the last lift-off in May 1973, all 13 Saturn V flights have been successful. Most famous was the launch on 16 July 1969, which carried the first men to land on the Moon, Neil Armstrong and Buzz Aldrin, with their co-astronaut Michael Collins.

## Eureka!

Apollo 13 was unlucky – an explosion damaged the oxygen supply. The crew had the idea to use the Lunar Module as a 'space lifeboat' until they went back to the Command Module for re-entry.

## Whatever next?

Will people ever go back to the Moon? The USA plans to send astronauts there again between 2015 and 2020.

*Russia's Energia rocket was slightly more powerful than Saturn V. However it only had two test launches and never went into full operation.*

**Second stage**  The S-II stage two had five J-2 rocket engines. It was 25 metres tall, and like the first stage, it was 10 metres wide.

*In 1973 the last Saturn V had rocket engines in two stages only. Its third stage was equipped as the Skylab orbiting space station.*

J-2 engines

**First stage**  The bottom part of the giant Saturn V was stage one, S-IC. It weighed more than 2000 tonnes (as much as 50 huge trucks) and was 42 metres tall.

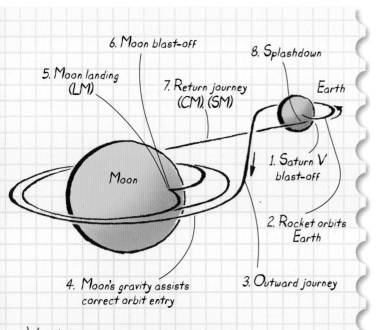

5. Moon landing (LM)
6. Moon blast-off
7. Return journey (CM), (SM)
8. Splashdown
Earth
Moon
1. Saturn V blast-off
2. Rocket orbits Earth
4. Moon's gravity assists correct orbit entry
3. Outward journey

## ✳ How does GRAVITY ASSIST work?

Not only the Earth has a pull of gravity. All objects do, from a tiny pinhead to planets, moons and stars. Spacecraft often fly near a moon or planet so its gravity pulls them around to head off in a new direction. This saves fuel and time on a long journey. On Apollo missions, planners had to take into account the Moon's gravity, which is one-sixth that of Earth's. The craft aimed to the side of the Moon as if going past it, then used the Moon's gravity assistance to pull it around into the correct orbit.

**F-1 engines**  Five F-1 rocket engines carried all three stages of Saturn V up to 60 kilometres before the first stage fell away.

*Three test Saturn Vs are on display at the Johnson Space Center, Houston, the Kennedy Space Center, Cape Canaveral and the Davidson Center, Huntsville.*

Watch amazing footage of the Saturn V launch and the first humans to set foot on the Moon by visiting www.factsforprojects.com and clicking on the web link.

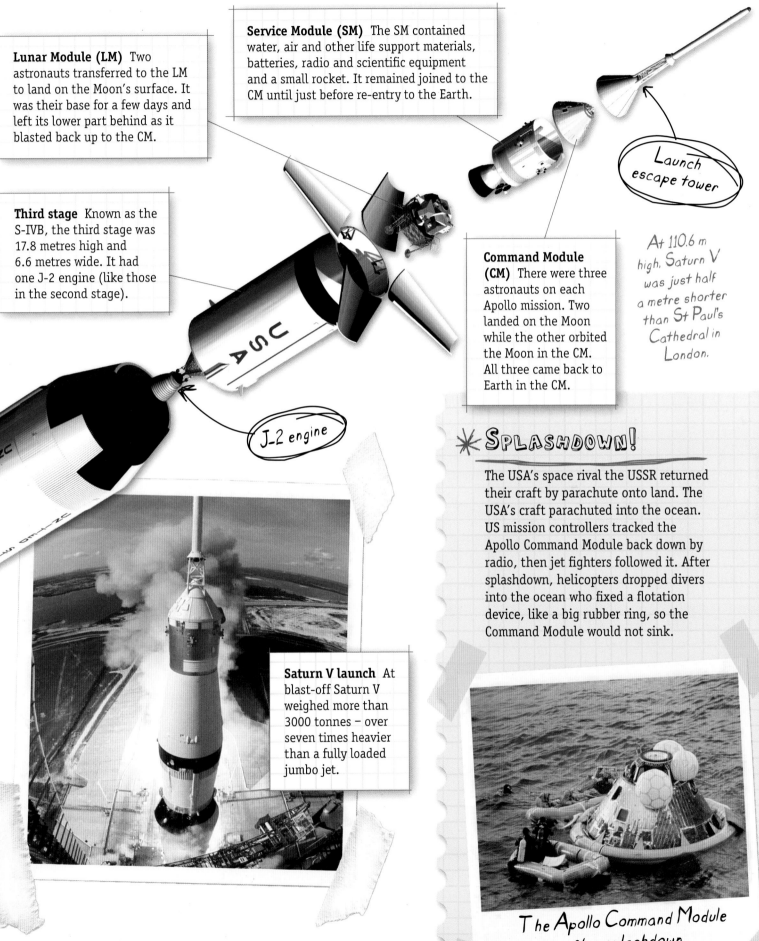

**Lunar Module (LM)** Two astronauts transferred to the LM to land on the Moon's surface. It was their base for a few days and left its lower part behind as it blasted back up to the CM.

**Service Module (SM)** The SM contained water, air and other life support materials, batteries, radio and scientific equipment and a small rocket. It remained joined to the CM until just before re-entry to the Earth.

Launch escape tower

**Third stage** Known as the S-IVB, the third stage was 17.8 metres high and 6.6 metres wide. It had one J-2 engine (like those in the second stage).

**Command Module (CM)** There were three astronauts on each Apollo mission. Two landed on the Moon while the other orbited the Moon in the CM. All three came back to Earth in the CM.

At 110.6 m high, Saturn V was just half a metre shorter than St Paul's Cathedral in London.

J-2 engine

## ✳ SPLASHDOWN!

The USA's space rival the USSR returned their craft by parachute onto land. The USA's craft parachuted into the ocean. US mission controllers tracked the Apollo Command Module back down by radio, then jet fighters followed it. After splashdown, helicopters dropped divers into the ocean who fixed a flotation device, like a big rubber ring, so the Command Module would not sink.

**Saturn V launch** At blast-off Saturn V weighed more than 3000 tonnes – over seven times heavier than a fully loaded jumbo jet.

The Apollo Command Module after splashdown

# PIONEER 11

Space probes are craft without crew, remote-controlled by radio signals from Earth. The twin probes Pioneer 10 and 11 were launched in 1972 and 1973 on vast journeys to fly past the outer planets millions of kilometres from Earth. They took pictures on the way and are still out there, heading away from Earth at incredible speeds into the unknown depths of space.

## Eureka!

After Pioneer 11's launch, mission controllers realized that they could use Jupiter's gravity to alter its course so that it would reach Saturn before two other probes, Voyagers 1 and 2.

*Pioneer 11 flew within 34,000 km of Jupiter and 21,000 km of Saturn.*

*In Pioneer 11's amazing pictures of Saturn's rings, the rings appeared dark. Yet when seen from Earth they are bright.*

Asteroid – Meteoroid detector senor

**Antenna dish** This bowl-shaped antenna was 2.74 metres across and pointed at Earth to send and receive radio signals.

Earth

Path of craft

*Spinning stabilizes craft as it travels*

## ✳ How does SPIN-STABILIZING work?

On its journey through space a craft might be hit by tiny particles called micrometeorites and start to wobble. This is why many satellites and probes are made to spin as they travel, known as spin-stabilizing. It causes them to fly straighter by the gyroscope effect (see page 32). Spinning also spreads out the heat of the Sun's rays, otherwise the side of the craft facing the Sun would become too hot (known as the 'barbeque effect'). Pioneer 11 spun around about once every 12 seconds but kept its dish pointing back to the Earth.

Separation ring

**Spin thrusters** Three pairs of small rocket thrusters controlled Pioneer's spinning motion and speed by puffing out jets of gas.

For information on all the Pioneer missions visit
www.factsforprojects.com and click in the web link.

Generator boom

Radioisotope generator

Earth lost touch with Pioneer 11 in 1995 and it's now heading toward the constellation (star group) Aquila, the Eagle. It should get there in about four million years!

Electric cable

**Main bus** The main body or bus of Pioneer 11 was almost 2 metres across. The 3-metre booms for the generators and the 6-metre magnetometer boom were folded up for launch and straightened in space.

**Magnetometer** The natural magnetic field of a planet gives clues to its structure. The magnetometer must be on a long arm (boom) away from the main body of the probe to avoid interference from the probe's electrical and magnetic equipment.

On its way to Jupiter, Pioneer 11 travelled 55 times faster than a high-power rifle bullet. It was accelerated to this speed by the gravity slingshot around Jupiter.

Magnetometer boom

**Thermal louvres** The covers on these long slots twisted and opened to let out heat when the electrical parts inside the probe got too warm.

As Pioneer 11 passed Saturn, its radio signals took more than one hour to reach Earth.

**Cosmic ray telescope** One of Pioneer 11's many instruments, the cosmic ray telescope looked at powerful cosmic rays travelling across the Universe.

✳ Is there ANYBODY out there?

Pioneer 11 was the second probe (after Pioneer 10) to reach Jupiter and the first to reach Saturn. Both Pioneers carry a plaque about 23 centimetres wide. This shows pictures of a man and woman, also the Solar System – our Sun and its planets – along the bottom and a chart of where the Earth is among the distant stars. In space the Pioneers will keep going for an immense time unless they hit a moon, a planet or an asteroid. Or maybe they will be found by aliens who perhaps can read the plaque and come to visit us!

Pioneer's plaque

# VOYAGER 2

In 1977, Voyagers 1 and 2 blasted off on vast journeys across the Solar System. Voyager 1 flew close to Jupiter and Saturn. Meanwhile Voyager 2 travelled more slowly to these planets, then headed onwards to become the first probe to visit Uranus and Neptune.

## Eureka!

Mission controllers forgot to switch on Voyager 2's main radio equipment because they were distracted by a problem with Voyager 1. Luckily there was a back-up radio.

## Whatever next?

The only probe that is planned to visit worlds beyond the outermost planet Neptune is New Horizons. It was launched in 2006 and should reach the 'dwarf planet' Pluto and its moon Charon in 2015.

**Cameras** Voyager 2 had two light-detecting cameras similar to those used by television crews. One took wide-view pictures and the other took narrow close-ups.

**Main bus** The bus or body of the probe was 1.8 metres across and 45 centimetres deep. It contained the main electronic equipment.

Cosmic ray detector

End cap

Heat shield

Radioactive fuel pellet

Casing contains wires of different metals

Cooling fins

Power outlet cable

## ✳ How do RADIOISOTOPE GENERATORS work?

In the depths of the Solar System, the Sun's light rays are too weak to power solar panels for electricity, and on a long trip lasting years, ordinary batteries would run out. So deep-space probes have radioisotope generators. These contain a pellet (lump) of plutonium fuel that is radioactive – it sends out energy in the form of particles and rays, including infrared (heat) rays. The heat warms wires of different metals, which are joined together to form a device called a thermocouple. This turns heat energy into electrical energy and has no moving parts so it lasts for years.

**Main antenna** The 3.7-metre dish received remote control commands from Earth and sent back pictures and other information as radio signals.

Voyager 2 flew within 81,000 km of Uranus and found ten unknown moons around the planet.

To see some of Voyager 2's stunning pictures of Saturn visit www.factsforprojects.com and click in the web link.

Voyager 2 is the only craft to visit Neptune. This planet will be far away from the probe New Horizons when when it crosses its orbit.

VOYAGER

JUPITER
SATURN
URANUS

Voyager 2's mission map

## ✳ GRAND TOUR

Voyager 2 is often called the 'best value' probe as it visited so many planets and moons and made important discoveries for a reasonable cost – about $500 million. Its 'Grand Tour' of outer planets was possible only because they were lined up in suitable positions, which happens once every 176 years. Voyager 2 made its closest approach to Jupiter in July 1979 and Saturn in August 1981. It used Saturn's gravity to 'slingshot' to Uranus in January 1986 and Neptune in August 1989. Both Voyager probes carried a gold-plated copper record (like an old vinyl record) with Earth pictures and sounds such as birds, whales, wind, thunder and people speaking.

**Magnetometer boom** This grid-like sensor detected magnetic fields of the various planets and moons that the probe passed, and the background magnetism of the Sun.

Scientists think that Voyager 2 will keep sending out radio signals until at least 2025, when it will be almost 50 years old.

Radioisotope generators

Voyager 2's twin, Voyager 1, is the most distant Earth-made object in space. It's travelling so fast that it will not be overtaken by any craft planned for the future.

**Long antennae** Two 10-metre whip-like aerials formed a V shape called the 'rabbit ears'. They listened for radio waves and other types of waves from deep space that give scientists clues to the origin of the Universe. The Voyagers' data is still being studied today.

# SPACE SHUTTLE

**R**ecycling is good for us and our planet – and most parts of the USA's space shuttles are recyclable. A space shuttle set-up consists of the white orbiter or 'spaceplane', two tall rocket boosters and a giant fuel tank. The first shuttle blasted off in 1981 and the last launch is expected soon after 2010, making a total of about 140 trips.

*Almost the whole orbiter re-entry is controlled by computer, except for lowering the landing wheels.*

## Eureka!

The shuttle's boosters produce more than two-thirds of lift-off thrust. To stop them hitting the orbiter as they separate or fall away, 16 very small rockets fire to push them clear.

**Cargo bay**  This large area for satellites, space telescopes and other payloads is 18 metres long and 5 metres wide – big enough to pack in a dozen family cars.

**Flight deck**  Like a big aircraft, the orbiter has two seats up front for the mission commander and the pilot.

*Cargo door*

*Orbiter*

## ☀ How do BOOSTERS work?

Boosters are additional rockets that give extra thrust for lift-off and other activities. The shuttle has two SRBs (Solid Rocket Boosters). When their fuel is used up, exploding bolts let them detach at a height of 45 kilometres. The empty casings parachute back down for re-use. At the mission's end the orbiter re-enters without engine power and swoops down to land on a runway like a huge glider.

*Hubble telescope carried in cargo bay*

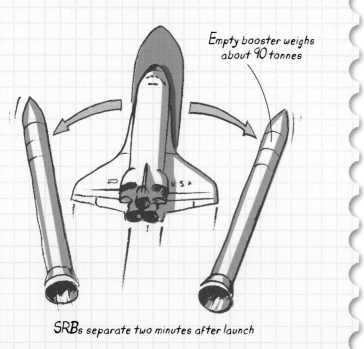

*Empty booster weighs about 90 tonnes*

*SRBs separate two minutes after launch*

**Main engines**
The orbiter has three RS-24 main engines. They can swivel slightly to direct their thrust and steer the craft.

*On the launch pad the whole space shuttle set-up is 56 m tall and weighs an incredible 2000 tonnes.*

## Whatever next?

After the space shuttles retire, the USA plans a two-stage rocket called Ares I. It will take a crew capsule, Orion, into space by 2015.

Learn everything you need to know about spacesuits by visiting www.factsforprojects.com and clicking on the web link.

The six orbiters are Enterprise (used for test landings), Discovery, Atlantis, Endeavour, Challenger (destroyed after lift-off in 1986) and Columbia (destroyed during re-entry in 2003).

Double-skin tank walls

**Fuel tank** The fuel tank is 46.9 metres tall and 8.4 metres wide. It supplies fuel to the three main orbiter engines. At take-off it weighs 755 tonnes and detaches from the orbiter after nine minutes.

Shuttles usually launch and land at Kennedy Space Center, Florida. In bad weather the orbiter can land at Edwards Air Force Base, California. It flies 'piggy-back' on a Boeing 747 jumbo jet for the 3500 km journey back to Florida.

## ✳ SPACE walking

Inside the orbiter, the crew wear normal clothes. To go outside they put on spacesuits. These contain air to breathe and protect them from intense glare in the Sun, freezing cold in shadow, and tiny bits of space dust called micrometeorites.

Liquid fuel

**Boosters** The SRBs (Solid Rocket Boosters) are 45.6 metres high and weigh almost 590 tonnes. They detach from the orbiter after two minutes.

The shuttle spacesuit is called the EMU, Extravehicular Mobility Unit

# MAGELLAN

In May 1989 the Magellan space probe blasted away from the space shuttle Atlantis, orbiting Earth on a 15-month journey. Its target was the planet next closest to the Sun from Earth – mysterious, cloud-shrouded Venus. In October 1994, after its hugely successful mission, controllers on Earth sent radio signals to Magellan instructing it to self destruct. It plunged down into Venus' thick poison clouds and burned away.

## Eureka!

The first space probe sent to Venus was the USSR's Venera 1 in 1961 but it lost radio contact with Earth. Finally, in 1962 Mariner 2 was the first probe to visit another planet when it flew within 35,000 kilometres of Venus.

## Whatever next?

The Venus Express probe reached Venus in 2006 (see page 32). A probe called VISE may carry the first lander to Venus, probably some time after 2015.

Once in Venus' orbit, with its rocket gone, Magellan was 4.6 m long.

**Solar panels** Two solar panels folded out after launch to provide enough electricity to power Magellan for five years.

The Magellan probe was named after explorer Ferdinand Magellan. He led the first round-the-world sailing voyage more than 500 years earlier (although he died on the way).

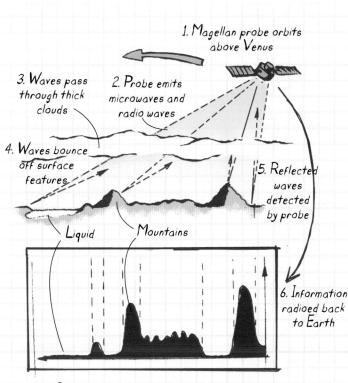

1. Magellan probe orbits above Venus

2. Probe emits microwaves and radio waves

3. Waves pass through thick clouds

4. Waves bounce off surface features

5. Reflected waves detected by probe

6. Information radioed back to Earth

Liquid    Mountains

7. Information used to make images showing surface height and nature of hard rock, loose dust or liquid

Propulsion module

**Rocket engine** The IUS (Inertial Upper Stage) solid fuel rocket burned several times to power Magellan away from Earth and towards Venus.

**Retrorocket** As Magellan neared Venus, its IUS rocket became a retrorocket. It slowed down the probe so that the planet's gravity could capture it into the correct orbit.

## ✳ How does RADAR work?

Shout at a distant wall and sound waves bounce off it and return as an echo. The time this takes shows the wall's distance. Radar is the same but with radio waves, microwaves or similar waves. Magellan sent out millions of microwave pulses and its antennae detected the reflections. The sooner these came back, the nearer the reflecting surface. The way the pulses changed as they reflected showed the nature of the surface.

For more amazing facts and stats about Magellan visit
www.factsforprojects.com and click on the web link.

**Low-gain antenna** This small dish helped the main antenna to send and receive radio signals, including those for radar mapping.

**High-gain antenna** The main 3.7-metre antenna (aerial) dish sent out microwaves for radar mapping and communicated by radio with Earth.

Altimeter antenna

**Star scanner** Star patterns were detected here so that Magellan could point in the correct direction, first to map part of Venus' surface, and then to aim the radio information back to Earth.

Magellan was the first deep-space probe to launch from a space shuttle.

Bus

**Thermal blanket** Most of Magellan's delicate electronic equipment was wrapped in a shiny covering. This reflected the Sun's heat and other rays, which are much stronger around Venus than on Earth.

Magellan was built from the spares and leftover parts of several other probes including the Voyagers and Galileo.

## ✳ RADAR VISION

Seen from Earth, Venus is covered by thick clouds. Magellan's radar signals passed through these clouds to reveal the hidden landscape below. The probe's inital orbit was lop-sided, ranging from over 8500 kilometres away from Venus to less than 300 kilometres. As it swooped low each time it made a narrow radar picture of a surface strip up to 28 kilometres wide and 70,000 kilometres long, from a different angle on each orbit.

Thousands of Magellan's radar images were used to make this picture of Venus

# HUBBLE SPACE TELESCOPE

In 1990 space shuttle Discovery took a massive payload into space – the HST, Hubble Space Telescope. The HST is still there today although only a few parts continue to work. Why take a bus-sized, 11-tonne telescope into an orbit 580 kilometres high? On Earth, even on a cloudless night, telescopes have to look through the blurry atmosphere. In space it's always dark and crystal clear.

People were planning space telescopes as early as the 1940s, but the HST was the first to be made.

## Eureka!

HST is named after US astronomer Edwin Hubble (1889–1953). He made the great discovery that the Universe is expanding as stars and galaxies fly away from each other an incredible speeds.

The central tube-shaped part of the HST is 13.2 m long and 4.2 m wide.

Door

**Secondary mirror** The smaller mirror is 30 centimetres across and weighs 12 kilograms.

**Solar panels** About 8 metres long, these turn sunlight into electricity to power all of the HST's equipment. They also charge batteries for the 36 minutes of each 97-minute orbit when the HST is in shadow, on the far side of the Earth from the Sun.

## ✳ How does the HST work?

The HST's optical (light-detecting) telescope is called a Cassegrain reflector. Light comes in through the open end door and bounces or reflects off the huge primary mirror, which curves inwards like a bowl. The light rays shine onto the secondary mirror, which curves outwards like a dome. It reflects them through a hole or aperture in the middle of the primary mirror, onto the scientific sensors and other instruments.

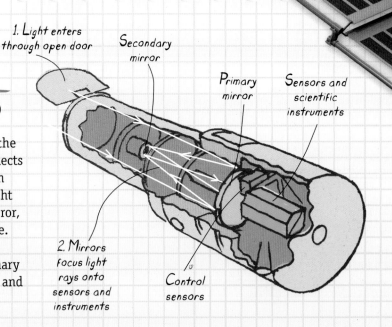

1. Light enters through open door

Secondary mirror

Primary mirror

Sensors and scientific instruments

2. Mirrors focus light rays onto sensors and instruments

Control sensors

## Whatever next?

Taking over from 'Hubble' should be 'Webb', the James Webb Space Telescope. Due for launch after 2012, it's main mirror will be about 6.5 metres across!

To watch videos, view galleries and read incredible facts about the Hubble visit www.factsforprojects.com and click on the web link.

Antenna

The HST has helped scientists to solve some of astronomy's big puzzles, such as how stars are born. However its other findings mean there are new mysteries about the size and shape of the Universe.

**Primary mirror** The main mirror that collects starlight is 2.4 metres across and weighs 830 kilograms. It took three years to cast, shape and polish.

The Hubble sees galaxies far away across the Universe

Reflective casing

### ✳ SHORT-SIGHTED TELESCOPE

Soon after launch, mission experts realized that the HST's view was slightly fuzzy – because its main mirror was not exactly the correct shape. In 1993 a space shuttle mission took astronauts and equipment to fix the problem. More shuttle missions in 1997, 1999 and 2002 serviced the equipment and made further improvements. Then from 2004, parts began to fail. The HST is slowly 'dying'.

Sun sensor

The HST zooms through space at almost 8 km every second.

Rear shroud

**Scientific instruments** Several sets of scientific equipment analyze the incredibly weak light and other waves coming in from deep space.

# CASSINI-HUYGENS

Saturn is our Solar System's second-biggest planet, sixth farthest from the Sun and famous for its glittering rings. In July 2004, two-part Cassini-Huygens was the fourth Earth craft to visit the planet. As the orbiter Cassini circled Saturn, the lander Huygens detached and touched down on Saturn's huge moon, Titan.

## Eureka!

Saturn's beautiful rings were first glimpsed by the great scientist Galileo Galilei in 1610 with his newly built telescope. He saw them only as vague bulges on either side of the planet and called them 'Saturn's ears'.

## Whatever next?

In 2011 the US plans to send a probe called Juno to Saturn's neighbour, Jupiter – which is also the biggest planet. It should arrive about five years after launch.

*Depending on the orbits of Earth and Saturn, radio signals can take more than 80 minutes to travel between us and Cassini.*

CASSINI

**Cameras** Cassini carries about 12 cameras and other scientific instruments. Some see visible light (like our eyes), others detect infrared (heat) and ultra-violet waves.

Parachute slowed decent

Heat shield prevented burn-up on entry, then detached

Large parachute and then smaller one slowed descent

Huygens lands on Titan

**Radar bay** Like Magellan (see page 24), Cassini uses radar based on radio waves to map the surface of Titan. It also 'listens' for natural radio signals coming from deep space.

## ✳ How do PROBES land?

On 25 December 2004, Huygens left Cassini and began its 21-day drift to huge Titan, which is half as big again as our own Moon. Unlike most other moons, Titan has an atmosphere of gases. During the descent through its atmosphere, Huygens was protected by a 2.7-metre heat shield or 'decelerator'. It was also slowed down by parachutes, first by a large one 8.3 metres across, then by a smaller 3-metre parachute. After two and a half hours, Huygens finally landed with a bump – still well and working.

**Power supply** Three radioisotope generators (see page 20) use radioactive plutonium fuel to make Cassini's electricity.

To build a model of the Cassini spacecraft visit
www.factsforprojects.com and click on the web link.

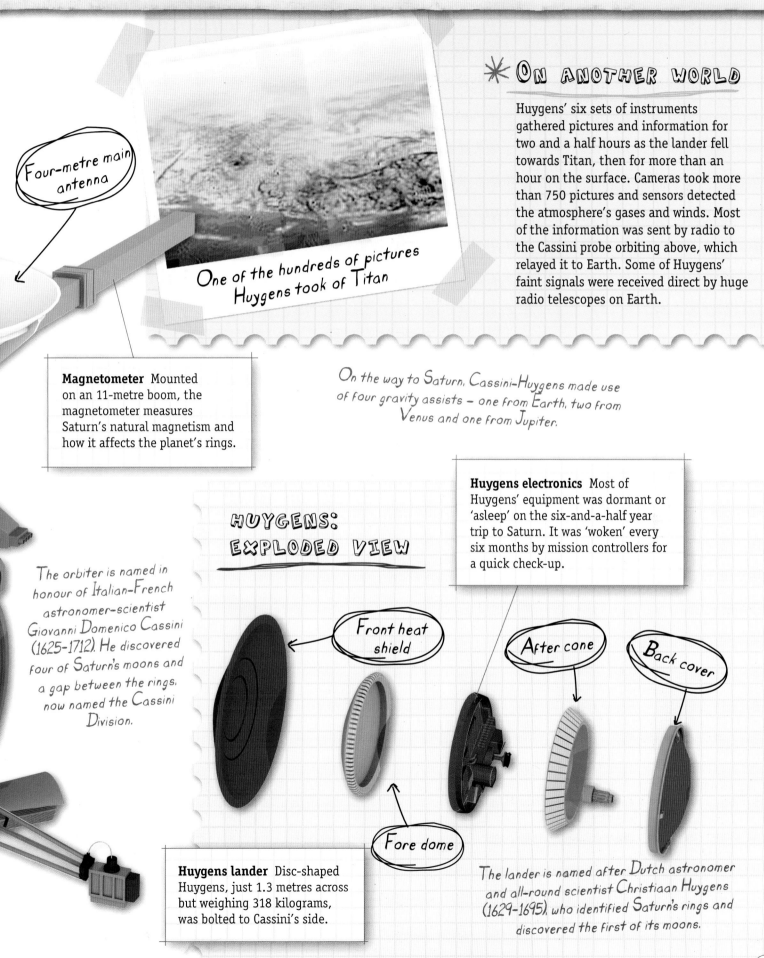

Four-metre main antenna

One of the hundreds of pictures
Huygens took of Titan

## ✳ ON ANOTHER WORLD

Huygens' six sets of instruments
gathered pictures and information for
two and a half hours as the lander fell
towards Titan, then for more than an
hour on the surface. Cameras took more
than 750 pictures and sensors detected
the atmosphere's gases and winds. Most
of the information was sent by radio to
the Cassini probe orbiting above, which
relayed it to Earth. Some of Huygens'
faint signals were received direct by huge
radio telescopes on Earth.

**Magnetometer** Mounted
on an 11-metre boom, the
magnetometer measures
Saturn's natural magnetism and
how it affects the planet's rings.

On the way to Saturn, Cassini-Huygens made use
of four gravity assists – one from Earth, two from
Venus and one from Jupiter.

**Huygens electronics** Most of
Huygens' equipment was dormant or
'asleep' on the six-and-a-half year
trip to Saturn. It was 'woken' every
six months by mission controllers for
a quick check-up.

## HUYGENS: EXPLODED VIEW

The orbiter is named in
honour of Italian-French
astronomer-scientist
Giovanni Domenico Cassini
(1625-1712). He discovered
four of Saturn's moons and
a gap between the rings,
now named the Cassini
Division.

Front heat shield

After cone

Back cover

Fore dome

**Huygens lander** Disc-shaped
Huygens, just 1.3 metres across
but weighing 318 kilograms,
was bolted to Cassini's side.

The lander is named after Dutch astronomer
and all-round scientist Christiaan Huygens
(1629-1695), who identified Saturn's rings and
discovered the first of its moons.

# SPIRIT AND OPPORTUNITY

**M**ore than half of all space missions to Mars have failed. Great successes were the USA's Mars Exploration Rovers, MERs. In June and July 2003 two rockets launched the twin rovers, which are remote-controlled robot vehicles. They landed on Mars three weeks apart in the following January. They have been trundling around since, taking pictures and gathering information.

## Eureka!

Mars has more spacecraft on its surface than any other planet, (apart from Earth) among them are:
- Mars 2 and 3 (1971)
- Vikings 1 and 2 (1976)
- Mars Pathfinder and its Sojourner rover (1997)
- Spirit and Opportunity
- Perhaps Beagle 2 (see page 33)
- Phoenix (2008, opposite)

## Whatever next?

Russia and China plan a mission called Phobos-Grunt to visit Mars' tiny moon Phobos and bring back samples of its rocks.

**Navcam** On the rover's mast are several cameras including two navcams to see rocks, boulders and hollows.

## How do PANCAMS work?

Twin panoramic cameras (mounted above the Navcam) on the rover's mast swivel and tilt to see a panoramic or all-around view. They detect shapes and colours in great detail. The two cameras look from slightly different angles, known as stereoscopic vision. From their two views the rover's computer can judge the distance of objects – just like our own eyes and brain.

Twin cameras give stereo vision

Tilt joint provides up and down movement

Swivel joint allows mast to rotate 360 degrees

**Solar panels** These produce electricity for up to four hours each Martian day (which is 37 minutes longer than an Earth day).

Surface radiator

**Mobile arm** The long arm carries five gadgets including a small camera for close-ups, magnets and a rock grinder.

The two rovers were named by nine-year-old Sofi Collins in an essay-writing competition.

Discover everything you need to know about Spirit and Opportunity by visiting www.factsforprojects.com and clicking on the web link.

**Front hazcam**
Two front and two rear hazard-avoidance cameras have a low, wide-angle view to see dangers such as small stones.

# Flight of the PHOENIX

Spirit and Opportunity are on opposite sides of Mars. Near the top of the planet, towards its North Pole, is another craft, the lander Phoenix. After a journey of 680 million kilometres from Earth it touched down in May 2008. It studies Martian dust and rocks with its robotic 2.3-metre drill-and-scoop arm. Two of its aims are to find out if there is, or was, water on Mars – and if there are signs of life.

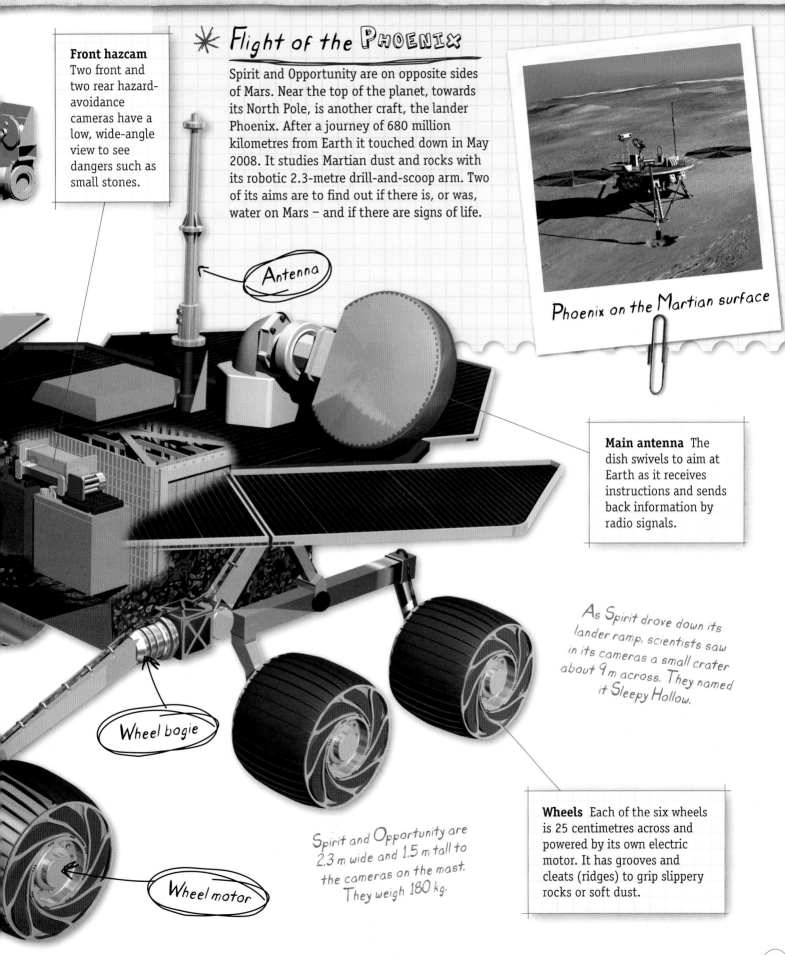

Phoenix on the Martian surface

Antenna

**Main antenna** The dish swivels to aim at Earth as it receives instructions and sends back information by radio signals.

As Spirit drove down its lander ramp, scientists saw in its cameras a small crater about 9 m across. They named it Sleepy Hollow.

Wheel bogie

Wheel motor

Spirit and Opportunity are 2.3 m wide and 1.5 m tall to the cameras on the mast. They weigh 180 kg.

**Wheels** Each of the six wheels is 25 centimetres across and powered by its own electric motor. It has grooves and cleats (ridges) to grip slippery rocks or soft dust.

# VENUS EXPRESS

Each spacecraft has a limited 'launch window' or time to blast off. This depends on many things such as if the weather is suitable for the rocket to leave, to whether the target planet or moon is in the best position from Earth. Venus Express almost missed this window. It left Earth in November 2005, nearly too late. However it still managed to get into Venus' orbit in May 2006.

## Eureka!

Venus Express has found out more about its planet's amazing 'greenhouse effect' due to all the carbon dioxide in its atmosphere ($CO_2$ is the main global warming gas here on Earth).

## Whatever next?

Japan plans a mission called Planet-C to Venus in the next few years. It will study the lightning storms and volcanoes there.

**Gold coat** Much of the probe is covered by a 23-layered sheet called MLI (Multi-Layer Insulation) to keep out the Sun's intense heat.

*Venus is by far the hottest planet in the Solar System. A warm day in midsummer can be 480°C!*

*Venus Express was developed from the Mars Express mission and uses many similar parts. It also has spare bits from the Rosetta probe, launched to study the comet Churyumov-Gerasimenko.*

**Solar panels** Venus is much closer to the Sun than the Earth is. The solar panels were carefully designed to cope with double the light energy, since Earth-type panels would overheat in the Sun's fearsome glare.

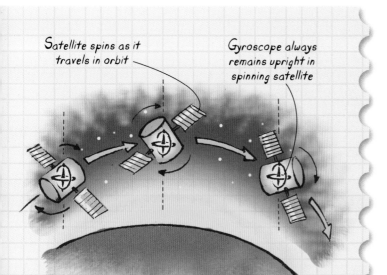

Satellite spins as it travels in orbit

Gyroscope always remains upright in spinning satellite

## ✳ How can GYROSCOPES help with control?

A moving object tends to keep going unless a force acts to slow it down or change its direction. A gyroscope is a heavy, very fast-spinning wheel or ball with great movement energy, so it resists being tilted or changing position. Inside a satellite, an electrical gyro whizzes around for years, staying in the same position even as the satellite around it spins or changes direction. Measuring the angle between the gyro and the satellite shows which way the satellite is pointing.

Read more about the Venus Express mission by visiting
www.factsforprojects.com and clicking on the web link.

**Antenna** The main 1.3-metre antenna studied the atmosphere of Venus and communicated with Earth.

The main body, or bus, of Venus Express is very small compared to similar probes – just 1.8 m long and 1.4 m high.

Gyros

**Rocket engine and thrusters** The main rocket engine burns to make big changes to the probe's path, as when slotting into orbit. Thrusters do small course corrections.

Many probes carry simple cameras called star trackers that detect pinpoints of starlight. From their patterns the on-board computer works out the probe's position, angle and course.

Positioning thrusters

## ✳ Lost in SPACE

In 1966 the USSR's Venera 3 was the first spacecraft to land on another planet – Venus. However all contact was lost, perhaps because it crash-landed or the planet's thick gases may have crushed it into a crumpled ball. In 2003 all contact was lost with Beagle 2 as it left its orbiter craft Mars Express for a landing on the surface. The fate of Beagle 2 is still a mystery. One day humans may arrive and find its smashed remains.

Beagle 2 as it should have landed

# SpaceShipOne

The X-Prizes are awards for great leaps forward in science and technology. In 1996 the Ansari X-Prize was offered for a craft able to carry three people into space twice in two weeks. However it had to be a private craft, built by a team of individuals or a company, not by a government or whole country. In 2004 SpaceShipOne, developed by Scaled Composites of California, USA, won the prize. Their reward – a cool $10 million.

## Eureka!

Pegasus was the first private (non-government) rocket, a solid-fuel rocket booster built by Orbital Sciences. In 1990 the first of its 40-plus launches took up two satellites. Unlike SpaceShipOne it never carried people.

## Whatever next?

SpaceShipOne was a forerunner of the much bigger SpaceShipTwo, the first 'spaceliner'. It is planned to carry passengers regularly on space trips and will be operated by Virgin Galactic.

SpaceShipOne retired soon after its spaceflights and is on display at the Smithsonian Institution's National Air and Space Museum in Washington DC, USA.

**Pilot** On its three space trips, SpaceShipOne carried just one person, the pilot, who didn't need to wear a spacesuit. The craft had enough room and power for three people.

Oxidizer tank

Porthole windows

**Controls** The pilot's controls were very similar to a small aircraft, with a control column or 'joystick' and two rudder pedals.

## ✳ How does FEATHERING work?

SpaceShipOne had a new way of slowing down and remaining steady during re-entry. The outer parts of its wings swung up, or 'feathered', so that the craft could come down at a steep angle with its heat-resistant underside facing the correct way. This also stopped SpaceShipOne from tilting or spinning. The wings swung back again for the final glide down and landing.

Rudders and elevons did not work in airless space

Steep angle of travel

Underside resisted heat of re-entry

Rear portion of tail boom rotated upwards

After gliding tests, the first powered trip of SpaceShipOne was 17 December 2003. This was exactly 100 years after the Wright brothers' first aircraft flight.

Watch the incredible flight of SpaceShipOne by visiting www.factsforprojects.com and clicking on the web link.

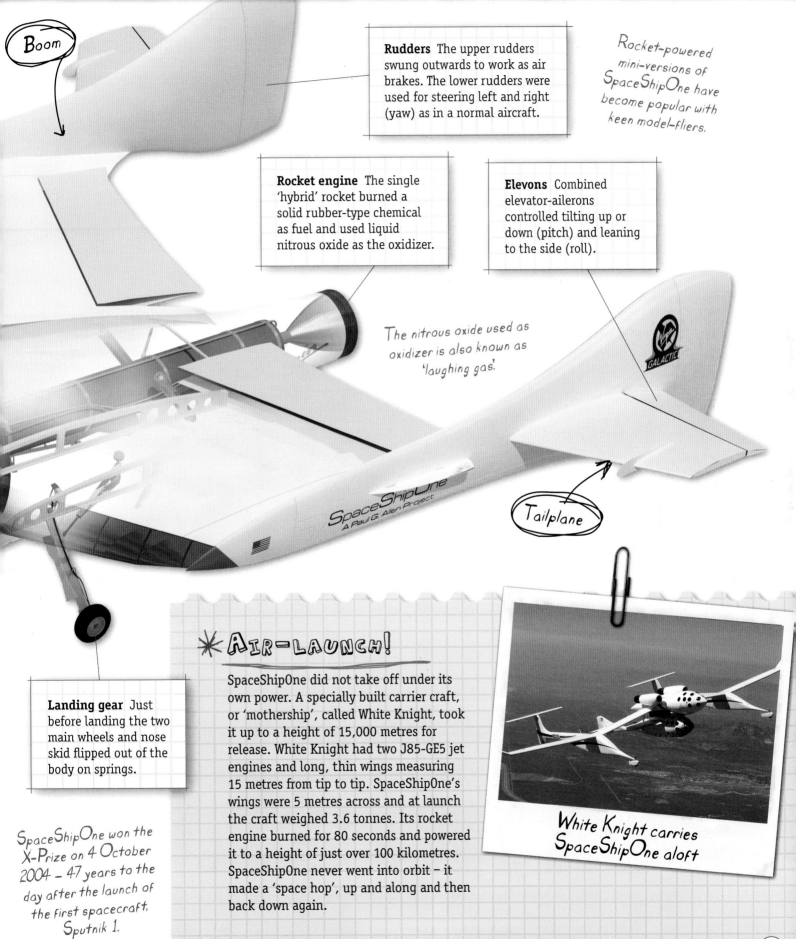

Boom

**Rudders** The upper rudders swung outwards to work as air brakes. The lower rudders were used for steering left and right (yaw) as in a normal aircraft.

Rocket-powered mini-versions of SpaceShipOne have become popular with keen model-fliers.

**Rocket engine** The single 'hybrid' rocket burned a solid rubber-type chemical as fuel and used liquid nitrous oxide as the oxidizer.

**Elevons** Combined elevator-ailerons controlled tilting up or down (pitch) and leaning to the side (roll).

The nitrous oxide used as oxidizer is also known as 'laughing gas'.

Tailplane

**Landing gear** Just before landing the two main wheels and nose skid flipped out of the body on springs.

SpaceShipOne won the X-Prize on 4 October 2004 – 47 years to the day after the launch of the first spacecraft, Sputnik 1.

## ✳ AIR-LAUNCH!

SpaceShipOne did not take off under its own power. A specially built carrier craft, or 'mothership', called White Knight, took it up to a height of 15,000 metres for release. White Knight had two J85-GE5 jet engines and long, thin wings measuring 15 metres from tip to tip. SpaceShipOne's wings were 5 metres across and at launch the craft weighed 3.6 tonnes. Its rocket engine burned for 80 seconds and powered it to a height of just over 100 kilometres. SpaceShipOne never went into orbit – it made a 'space hop', up and along and then back down again.

White Knight carries SpaceShipOne aloft

# INTERNATIONAL SPACE STATION

The first space stations in orbit around Earth where people could stay for days or weeks, were the USSR's Salyut series from 1971 and the USA's Skylab in 1973. Much bigger was Russia's Mir, which lasted from 1986 until it burned up (without crew) on re-entry in 2001. The only current space base is the International Space Station, ISS. Building began in 1998 and will finish around 2010.

## Eureka!

The ISS began as an idea to combine three separate planned space bases – USA's Freedom, Russia's Mir-2 and the European Space Agency's Columbus.

## Whatever next?

The ISS is planned to stay in service until at least 2016. Next could be a Moon base, possibly finished around 2025.

*The ISS travels at 27,700 km/h and completes almost 16 orbits every 24 hours.*

## ✳ How do SOLAR PANELS work?

A solar panel, or array, has thousands of button-sized PV (photovoltaic) cells. Each takes in the energy of sunlight and changes it into electricity. The electric current is fed through a control unit to batteries. These charge up during half of each orbit when the ISS is on the sunny side of Earth, for use during the other half.

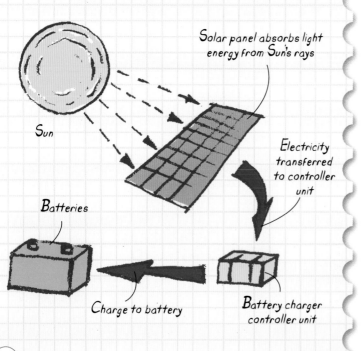

Solar panel absorbs light energy from Sun's rays

Sun

Electricity transferred to controller unit

Batteries

Charge to battery

Battery charger controller unit

Airlock

**Soyuz** There is always at least one Russian Soyuz spacecraft docked at the ISS as a 'lifeboat' in case of an emergency, such as crew illness. Soyuz takes almost two days to launch and chase after and link onto the station, but it can be back down on Earth in less than four hours.

*The ISS has an elliptical (oval) orbit at a height of between 275 and 425 km. It can be seen from Earth with the unaided eye, if you know where to look!*

For a complete guide to the International Space Station
visit www.factsforprojects.com and click on the web link.

# ✳ Life SUPPORT

All the basics of life must be taken up to the ISS by spacecraft such as the USA's space shuttles, Russia's Soyuz (with crew) and Progress (without crew), and Europe's Jules Verne (another 'robot' craft without crew). Supplies include water, food and even air to breathe. However there is plenty of recycling. Filters clean the air and an Elektron machine makes fresh oxygen from water. In fact all the water from the shower, sink, astronaut's breathed-out air and even their urine is re-used – after cleaning, of course.

A state-of-the-art toilet on board the ISS

**Canadarm2** This remote-control arm, nearly 18 metres long, runs on rails along the main truss. It moves equipment and even space-walking astronauts.

**Solar panels** Also called photovoltaic arrays, the solar panels swivel as the ISS orbits so they point at the Sun. Each panel is about 34 metres long.

**Main truss** The truss is the 'backbone' of the ISS to which all the other modules and parts are fixed. It is made up of about 12 sections called segments with code names such as S1 and P6.

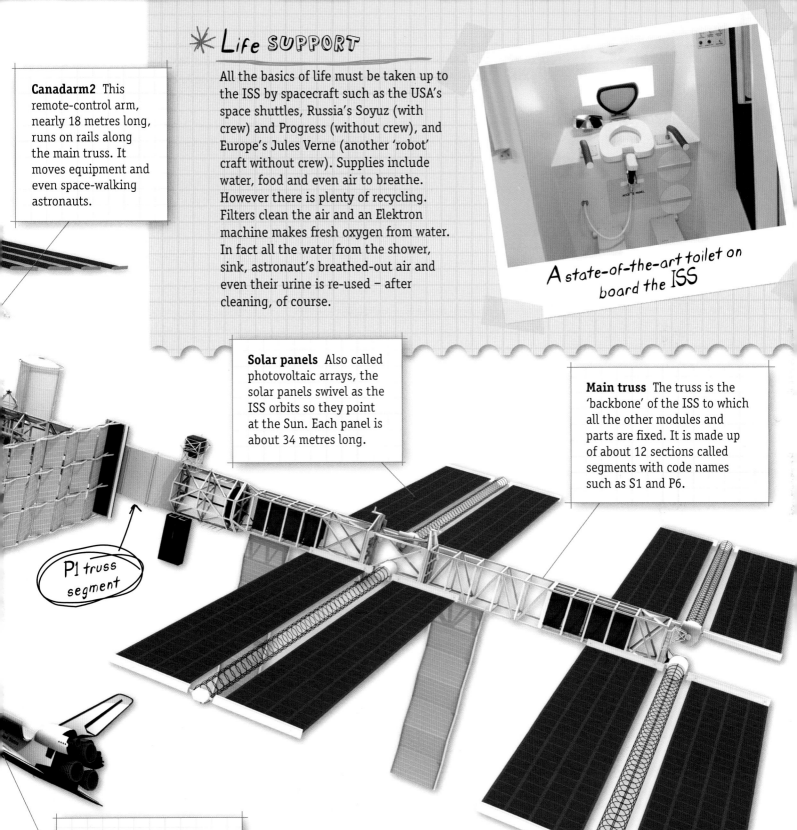

P1 truss segment

**Space shuttle** Visiting spacecraft join the ISS at docking ports. The connection is airtight so that the crew can enter the ISS through an airlock.

The ISS sinks downwards about 2000 m each month. It has to be pushed back up again using small booster rockets on its visiting spacecraft.

# GLOSSARY

## Antenna
Part of a communications system that sends out and/or receives radio signals, microwaves or similar waves and rays. Most antennae (also called aerials) are either long and thin like wires or whips, or dish-shaped like a bowl.

## Atmosphere
The layer of gases around a very large space object such as a planet. It fades with height into the nothingness of space.

## Booster
An added-on rocket that gives extra thrust, for example, when blasting off from a planet's surface, or when leaving an orbital path to travel into deep space.

## Bus
The main body or central part of a craft such as a space probe or satellite, to which the other parts and modules are attached.

## Combustion chamber
A chamber where fuel burns (combusts) to produce roaring, high-pressure hot gases, as in a rocket engine.

## Elevon
The control surface of a tail-less or 'flying wing' aircraft or spacecraft, which is a combined elevator and aileron.

*Gyroscope stability*

## Escape velocity
The minimum speed or velocity needed to leave the pull of gravity of an object and escape into space.

## Gravity
The natural pulling force or attraction that all objects have, no matter what their size. Bigger or more massive objects have more gravity than smaller ones.

## Gyroscope
A device that maintains its position and resists being moved or tilted because of its movement energy, usually consisting of a fast-spinning ball or wheel.

## Heat shield
A special part of a spacecraft made to absorb and resist the heat of entry or re-entry as the craft comes from space into an atmosphere.

## Infrared
A form of energy, as rays or waves, which is similar to light, but with longer waves that have a warming or heating effect.

## Launch vehicle
The part of a space mission that launches the payload and other parts, lifting them up into space – usually called the 'rocket'.

## Launch window
The limited time when a space mission can take off. Before and after this time period the mission will no longer be possible, for example, because its target planet is too far away.

## Lunar
To do with a moon, usually the Moon (Earth's moon).

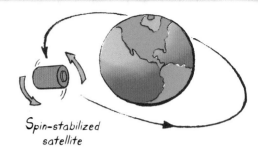

*Spin-stabilized satellite*

## Magnetometer
A scientific instrument that detects magnetic forces, such as the natural magnetic fields of planets.

## Module
A main part or section of a spacecraft, for example, containing all the radio equipment, or the batteries, or housing scientific instruments such as telescopes.

## Moon
A space object that orbits a planet, like Titan orbiting Saturn. 'The' Moon (with a capital M) travels around the Earth.

## Multi-stage rocket
A rocket or launch vehicle with several sections that fire or burn one after the other, falling away when their fuel is used up.

## Nozzle
A device through which the flow of gases and liquids are controlled, as in a rocket engine or thruster.

## Optical telescope
A telescope that works using light rays, instead of other waves or rays (such as radio waves).

## Orbit
A curved path around a larger object, such as a spacecraft going around Earth, or the Earth orbiting the Sun. Orbits can be circular, elliptical ('oval'), teardrop-like and other shapes.

## Payload

The load or cargo part of a space mission, such as a satellite or space probe, as opposed to the launch vehicle or rocket that takes it up into space.

## Planet

A very large space object that orbits a star, like the eight planets, including Earth, orbiting the Sun.

## Probe

A craft without crew that is remote-controlled from Earth, which usually undertakes a long-distance deep-space mission.

## Radar

A system for detecting the presence of objects by sending out radio waves, which reflect, or bounce off, an object back to the source.

## Radio telescope

A telescope that works using radio waves, microwaves or similar waves, instead of the light rays detected by an optical telescope.

## Radioisotope generator

A device that turns the radioactive energy (rays) given off by certain substances into electricity.

## Re-entry

When a spacecraft comes back into the layer of gases (atmosphere) around a planet or moon.

## Retrorocket

A rocket engine that fires to slow down a spacecraft, for example, as it enters orbit or touches down on a planet or moon.

Radioisotope generator

## Return mission

A space trip where the craft comes back to its starting place, usually Earth, rather than travelling away into deep space.

## Rocket

A type of engine or motor that burns fuel using oxygen or an oxygen-rich chemical (oxidizer). It produces a blast of hot gases that provide a force called thrust.

## Rover

In space, a wheeled vehicle that can travel around and explore, such as the lunar rovers used by astronauts on the Moon, or the remote-controlled Spirit rover on Mars.

## Rudder

The control surface of an aircraft or spacecraft, usually on the upright fin or 'tail', that makes it steer left or right (yaw).

## Satellite

Any object that goes around or orbits another. For example, the Moon is a natural satellite of the Earth. The term is used especially for artificial or man-made orbiting objects, particularly those going around the Earth.

## Solar

To do with the Sun.

## Solar panel

A device that turns sunlight directly into electricity, as used on many satellites and near-space probes.

## Space station

A base in space, usually orbiting a planet, where people can stay to live and work for weeks, months or even years.

SpaceShipOne

## Star

A huge space object that gives out heat and light. The nearest star to Earth is the Sun.

## Thrust

A force that pushes an object forwards, such as the rocket blast that moves a spacecraft.

## Thruster

A small nozzle or jet-like part that squirts or puffs out gases, usually to make small adjustments to a spacecraft's position or its direction of travel.

## Tracking station

A place with a large radio receiver, such as a dish, which detects radio waves or similar signals from a spacecraft and follows or tracks its course.

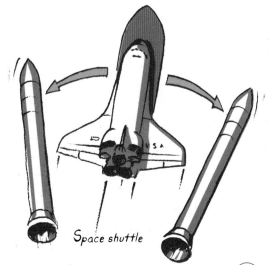

Space shuttle

# INDEX